PRESSURES OF AUTOIMMUNITY

by Karen Kellock Ph.D.

Manual for Superior Men

A complete theory based on Einstein physics,
Political Psychology, Systems Theory
and Archetypal Psychiatry.

FORMULA

All success attraction
All disease obstruction
All recovery elimination

You must fast on all three

OBSTRUCTIONS:

People
Habit
Food

PRESSURES OF AUTOIMMUNITY

If you don't feel safe and loved as number One like a baby in the arms of mom then drop the bum.   People are cruel so hold your head up high: the better you are the more they'll attack the fine.   People go thru rough patches and all men are sinners--that's what you tell wicked accusers. Forgiveness breaks their influence finally--before then you're yoked see. Life is a ladder and when older you're far more protected, not so naive like before.

DETOX FOR THE MAX

THEY THOUGHT YOU WERE LOW
MEANT TO SHINE BRIGHT
GOD BROUGHT IT ALTOGETHER
NEW POT SUX: POTHEADS IN DETOX
A RACING HEART & WEED SHAKES
BAD TRIPS ON HIGH THC
CHANGE OF PERSONALITY
NEW AVENUES OPEN UP
EVERYTHING RETURNS TO NORMAL
SENSE OF TASTE COMES BACK
DAILY RENEWAL/SPRING IN STEP
THEY FIDDLED WITH POT
FUTURE IS POSITIVE NOW
RAPID DECREASE OF ANXIETY
WHEN BRAIN AND HEART HEALS
ELIMINATING IT ALL FOR GOOD

DETOX FOR THE MAX

THEY THOUGHT YOU WERE LOW

They never expected you to elevate to the next level, they felt superior so acted like the devil.

Be happy these people are removed from your life and when they try to hoover you back, deny.

Just as you had a season of treason you will now have a season of success so wait, it's coming sis.

They threw so much dirt on your name you turned out a celebrity. They weren't expecting that see.

Even on your worst days you look your best cuz you've so improved yourself it's embedded sis.

You're it man, and the whole neighborhood can see it. There's something so different they intuit.

MEANT TO SHINE BRIGHT

You were meant to shine bright but they eclipsed and cut out your light yet now you're back, aye!

By them deleting you from family or group it made you stand out more, focusing on your goals too.

Rejecting and throwing mud on your name caused you to compensate--ELEVATE--and it is great.

By them coming to destroy you they actually helped to promote you/make you a better person too.

God used you to shed light on people like that, and to never go back because you've learned fast.

DETOX FOR THE MAX

When they start running their numbers on you, and you take it up to a point but then split it's cool.

They wake up thinking: "today is the day I'm gonna mess with their head" so drop em instead.

They thought so low about you they can't believe you're a celebrity now and it's stuck in their craw.

GOD BROUGHT IT ALTOGETHER

God's omniscience used all bad events in life to shape you into the man/woman you are today, aye.

A man wanting to impress/be with you won't do a thing to offend you so reject any disrespect Sue.

A woman won't leave a man if he provides for, protects and treats her with kindness: no way sis.

My husband provides for, protects and treats me with kindness [giving me privacy is a bonus].

An alpha male WANTS to provide for, protect and respect his chosen lady with kindness sis.

Seven out of ten divorces initiated by women. Does this indicate it is the man who is the problem?

NEW POT SUX: POTHEADS IN DETOX

Living with the pain of not being a speaker was never better by smoking a joint, just a depressor.

People who've happily smoked pot for 50 years are now having panic attacks as its 400% stronger!

THC in pot has gone from 4% to 30% lately and smokers are going into hospitals or calling emergency.

DETOX FOR THE MAX

Don't get me wrong, I loved it for years. But I would not try it again--even a puff--for a million dollars.

The "weed shakes" lasted days with panic attacks, repeating again just from recalling back.

The hospitals and fire stations are overloaded from potheads storming in after having it.

It's psychological: your vitals may be fine. But the hellish thoughts you'll have to wait out, aye.

A RACING HEART & WEED SHAKES

The racing heart/fibulations are such a total scare any potheads continuing to smoke is rare.

If you wanna smoke pot for healing, grow it yourself. 4% THC and 7% CBD would be gentle enough.

After loving the stuff this was hard to take. It was a mainstay but I had to find a different way.

Every time the urge came to mind I'd say "NO" recalling what just happened--don't forget it now.

No alcohol, coffee, pot, jet pills or chocolate. Guess that makes me a saint, don't you know it?

Hospitals can't treat the sick cuz so many potheads are coming in from a terrifying/dangerous trip.

I've had it. I've smoked since my twenties and anxious to start a brand new sparkling journey.

I could never conger that my own reality would be as exciting and creative as being stoned see.

I always saw POT as an entry to a new world. Now I see my God-given inner reality is what I want sir.

DETOX FOR THE MAX

No one who loves America would ever think of legalizing **HIGH THC WEED** but Biden wants to see.

BAD TRIPS ON HIGH THC

Bad trips from strong weed are clogging hospitals and fire stations so they can't attend to sick ones.

Many people including myself faced death from the bad effects and they quit right away they said.

Bad trips from edibles are truly horrible and smoking it is having the same effect: incredible.

Pot damages the brain and the heart. God gave me a good brain so I no longer see it as a lark.

Stimulants and pot, pot and stimulants: this is the new age that caught us and it was sinfulness.

What about bong lung--the productive cough. Everyone hates it but it will be gone soon enough.

Let's talk about orality, the motion of smoking. It's so habitual but wasn't there from the beginning.

CHANGE OF PERSONALITY

Habitual smoking changed the personality. Any bad habit does so anticipate your old one see.

Anticipate reversion to your happy, loving, cute self after this long, dangerous trip into hell.

God didn't create us to smoke dope all day then recover our breathing from a nebulizer, no way.

Those are chances we take when addiction's involved but success will come cuz our God loves.

DETOX FOR THE MAX

God wants us to be as He made us ok? Not smoking all day, come on: we always knew that anyway.

Stop drugs & watch new avenues open up--FINALLY. You always wondered what the block was see.

I couldn't take edibles so it had to be smoke. It ages the skin so regain beauty by becoming unyoked.

Stop being a smoking machine--whether pot or nicotine--and success comes suddenly.

NEW AVENUES OPEN UP

As soon as I stopped new avenues opened up. It was as if God was waiting for His child to grow up.

I gave up pot, albuterol, jet pills, coffee and chocolate and God said your time has come, dig it.

I loved pot more than anything. That's how this is a big thing but a brand new sane life is everything.

I was so sick from my life of pot I now relied/lived on melons, grapes, citrus and beef broth.

After your detox & rejuvenation you can go to the gym, make new friends and really live again.

Hear the birds, smell the flowers, renew friendship with neighbors, learn to cook, become a dancer.

Good luck in quitting smoking. Your baseline [who you are] will now return to normalcy and quickly.

EVERYTHING RETURNS TO NORMAL

Everything returns to normal within weeks as a loving God forgives and gives you all you seek.

DETOX FOR THE MAX

Though you smoked day and night for years, your poor heart and brain are restored, free of fears.

The decision to stop smoking is the beginning of a transformative health journey, glowing.

The mere desire for a healthier life initiates a series of handsome changes in body and mind.

It's a challenge but so rewarding as the changes occur in body, mind and life- and success is coming.

SENSE OF TASTE COMES BACK

Within weeks the sense of taste comes back. I can't believe how delicious it all tastes: fact.

In detox use beef broth with butter. Add scallions and little carrots and optimism returns brother!

Also in detox take melons, citrus, avocados and grapes. Now your health will jump back first rate.

As you overcome desire and the days go on, you feel so much accomplishment and joy: keep on!

Suddenly you have "found time" from the lack of pot paraphernalia: screens/pipes/papers/tar etc.

Suddenly you have a clear desk with nothing but pens and papers and plans for the future.

Pot causes mucus production and a gross cough. That's all gone now and friends feel more love.

I'll never forget the gasping for breath. A life so uncomfortable and for what? death?

I relish in my new health and comfort. The amazing thing is a surge of energy: now I come first.

DETOX FOR THE MAX

I never could take a deep breath without coughing. It's such a delight to breath now--just amazing!

I had already quit alcohol years back. It was a worse fate always putting me in disgrace, in fact.

These are the hip diseases of civilization: stimulants, downers and delicious killers of persons.

But food isn't delicious with these things. Become pure and true delight you'll REALLY feel and see.

DAILY RENEWAL/SPRING IN STEP

With each passing day I am renewed with a spring in my step and a joy in my heart free of defects.

This new vitality is a powerful invigorator and you can't believe how you postponed it for years.

Enthusiasm and confidence you will all get back. A child of God again not an addict and wreck.

The thirty day mark is a monumental achievement. Now you'll feel a plethora of physical benefits.

It's not just breathing easier but lung capacity increases so every breath brings joy like earlier years.

Skin takes on a healthy glow not looking old. And lung issues fade away, replaced by new goals.

When lung capacity expands each breath feels so invigorating you know it's designed by divinity.

Your body is healing, your vitality is returning, and with each passing day the future is more enticing.

Our bodies WANT to eliminate these toxins but only if we're stoppin'. Keep smokin' & they're stayin'.

DETOX FOR THE MAX

The sweats usually last for two days. Keep putting the beef broth in and enjoy fruit otherwise ok.

On the third day things took a turn. There was a "click" and things reversed I began to discern.

For Type A people who were always working, pot was a nice break while continuing creating.

All over the world people are taking a break with pot. Tho' common as liquor now, watch out.

After about a week in bed soaked with sweat I began to feel quite good again--really, like a little kid.

THEY FIDDLED WITH POT

They've fiddled with the pot strains so much it's more of a synthetic. Thank God I no longer trust it.

The detox on so many things simultaneously was rough but this accomplishment made me tough.

Sitting at your desk you want to smoke. See instead your new skin and energy, being unyoked.

I couldn't take edibles so it had to be smoke. It ages the skin so regain beauty by becoming unyoked.

Extension of circulation and overall heart health is the greatest boost. You feel natural energy too.

The rapid transformation in blood circulation feels like a miracle when every puff made you miserable.

The longer you remain smoke free the larger and more enduring these benefits so now just get fit.

Pumping oxygen rich blood throughout the body with increased efficiency feels simply heavenly.

DETOX FOR THE MAX

Hello to a smoke free, heart healthy life of increased abundance as you see more evidence.

Lung disease, heart attacks and stroke--all from the smoke--are DRASTICALLY reduced folks.

Research shows a "significant increase of longevity following cessation" and you want this son.

Continuing abstinence requires new habits or routines. Start building a new body or take up painting.

FUTURE IS POSITIVE NOW

The future after quitting are overwhelmingly positive. Your destiny has arrived, no more negative.

God is watching and now pours down blessings that have been blocked by this habitual craving.

Smoke-free days enjoying delicious food you can now taste gives you a healthy future, top rate.

This journey's challenging but the benefits are overwhelming, adding years to your life finally.

Things like PTSD and grudges from the past dissolve. The smoke kept us obsessed with em I'm told.

The FOUND TIME from quitting pot is the best part. You get so much of life back not just the heart.

My entire outlook and perception changed not being high all the time. A child's happy view, aye.

I thought it was helping anxiety and stress levels. Now I found out it just made me a nervous devil.

RAPID DECREASE OF ANXIETY

DETOX FOR THE MAX

When I stopped my anxiety rapidly decreased to be replaced by real life and I was amazed.

All those panic attacks in emergency rooms and fire stations were from POT: how embarrassin'.

As a lecturer I couldn't do my job anymore in fear of a coughing outbreak beyond my control.

Low self-esteem is inevitable when using a crutch. You know inside it's wrong & it reflects a bunch.

Self-confidence bursts open when you know you're finally doing what is needed and it shows.

WHEN BRAIN AND HEART HEALS

When the brain heals you have so much hope for the future, not feeling you're gonna die sooner.

The sense of accomplishing quitting a destroyer of life starts brand new endeavors & goals, aye!

You think you need pot to survive even tho it has been making all your problems worse, aye.

Addicted to the religion of marijuana is a disconnection from SELF so now your social life opens up.

After quitting the quality of friends changes dramatically. This is the biggest boost, truly.

I now choose to be with people with common futures not common pasts--those are gone at last.

Day three: sweating! It's addiction leaving your body which recalibrates to normal finally.

Your dopamine deficit from pot smoking will be replaced by friends, money and creativity.

DETOX FOR THE MAX

All addiction are loss of control over mind, behavior and decisions. Now we act right with commitment.

We thought pot calmed PTSD. But when you stop comes night terrors on the second day see.

You've insomnia waking up in a deep sweat. That's not just detox but unblocked PTSD instead.

ELIMINATING IT ALL FOR GOOD

Suddenly I couldn't handle a whole host of things: chocolate, pot, coffee, jet pills--all scary.

It all triggered the limbic system and I'd go psychotic with terror and sadness, utter madness.

When you're as high wired as I am you're thrown over by every little thing. Repent for real winning.

Coffee gave me a delightful surge at age 16 but at my age now it triggers and is a terrifying thing.

Maybe the low energy types can take these stimulants that have always been with us but I can't sis.

I'm born high wired to be a great orator but was held back by whatever so I had to repent of it all sir.

The liberal elite are always insulated from the crises they create, being behind their fancy gate.

PRESSURES OF AUTOIMMUNITY

PRESSURES OF AUTOIMMUNITY

IT'S NOT BRAVE TO COLLECTIVELY GANG UP
DEMOCRATS DON'T CARE ABOUT CRIME OR PEOPLE
THE DEVIL OR THE SYSTEM?
THE COMMUNIST SPIRIT IS FAKE EMPATHY
THEY MOCK AND SCOFF AT YOUR VIEWS
BEST BECOMES WORST, WORST BECOMES BEST
GOD'S PECULIAR PEOPLE
WHEN THE LAST CHRISTIAN DIES
IT WAS GOOD I WAS BASHED: THINK THAT
THINGS MUST GET WORSE TO GET BETTER
DEPENDENCY BRINGS FORCED REMOVAL
ON THOSE NOT SEEING A NEED FOR WALLS
BONDS AND TRIGGERS OF OLD SYSTEMS
FAVOR IS THE ESTABLISHED TIME
FORGET MAN, GOD DOES THE LIFTING
YOU HAD TO GO THRU IT *ALL!*
MUST SPEAK TRUTH TO REPROBATE MINDS
TRUTH NOT BASED ON FANS AND FOLLOWERS
CYCLES ALL THRU HISTORY
A BRAND NEW WORLD WITHOUT LOGIC
NOT BORN THAT WAY
GOD'S JUDGMENT FRIGHTENING AS IT FALLS ON A COUNTRY
GLYCATION DIET FOR VANITY
AUTOIMMUNE REACTIONS TO FOODS
NO GRAINS, DAIRY, NIGHTSHADES, CITRUS, LAND ANIMAL
KIDS ARE RIGHT TO HATE VEGGIES
AUTOIMMUNE REACTIONS TO EGGS OR DAIRY
AUTOIMMUNE REACTIONS TO STARCH
TOTAL LOAD AND AUTOIMMUNITY
TO THE ART AND SCIENCE DISCOVERERS

PRESSURES OF AUTOIMMUNITY

If you don't feel safe and loved as **NUMBER ONE** like a baby in the arms of mom drop the bum.

I don't want any trouble and don't wanna feel vulnerable. I'm getting quieter, in a bubble.

Life's too short for this crap. The minute you feel so one-upped you must withdraw or stay mad.

People are cruel so hold your head up **HIGH**. The better you are the more they'll attack the fine.

These are lessons I've learned in the school of hard knocks or a Ph.D. in the Streets with thugs.

So get hep, learn to rely on God not these clods, learn to love solitude and yourself, so mod!

God doesn't want you doing things you've been doing and listen carefully: He finds it disgusting.

START AT THE BEGINNING

People go thru rough patches and all men are sinners. That's what you tell your wicked accusers.

They're acting like lunatics and we've got to stop it. We must stop it now. President Donald Trump

Stop remorsing over the demon that was in you. Is he gone now? It's also like he never was too.

It was so traumatic trying to adapt to the Dunning-Kruger Effect when you're the Elect.

PRESSURES OF AUTOIMMUNITY

It was a mistake, a one-shot deal--but they make an entire history of it but not when they fall.

See forgiveness as one thing: breaking their influence finally. Before then you're yoked honey.

Stop resenting him as an unwanted visitor and start seeing him as a hated/criminal invader.

Being single is being exposed. Being married is coming behind wonderful, protective and happy walls.

Praise in public, reprimand in private. That's a good rule to follow for any true leader and I like it.

Life is a ladder and when you're older you're far more protected dear, not so naive like you were.

PROTECT YOUR HEART

Protect your heart too: don't get so involved. Keep your head, don't fall in love like a puppy dog.

You've got YOUR thing, your work, your creative days on earth. Don't get so involved, it's a curse.

Every time I got involved it was like going down an evil rabbit hole. Third parties, we avoid em all.

It wasn't that you were "bad" just arrogant in overreach so then the world came back hard see.

Don't call em "pre-convict teens" but what they are--criminals who are most dangerous by far.

Always go forward, don't look back. For we are all sinners who've made mistakes in fact.

I'm done talking about sibling abuse and narcissism. I'm just so darn glad I got away from them.

PRESSURES OF AUTOIMMUNITY

What they blamed me for was in their filthy minds. That's always how it is with human kind.

If to deal with abuse you go into denial like I did you'll have to pay the piper later/remember it.

Stress hormones are chronic from childhood neglect, like when the father's gone or mom's sick.

You don't conform, we blow your brains out in the town's square while everyone watches: beware.

In terror she escaped to the arms of any man around too scared and dense to correct the error.

Not only did God remove the hedge I was cast out from the homestead exposed and molested.

LOOKING AROUND FOR A CRUTCH

I looked around for a crutch and found nothing much but alcohol and drugs, attracting thugs.

God didn't want me to drink and to teach me, the minute i picked it up in came treachery.

Any crutch to deal with anxiety turned on me instantly. Food, booze or leaning on bad company.

As I matured I saw fasting [on anything] worked miracles not taking in substances see.

Two different worlds. I was always happy when I was eating but now not, only when fasting.

Instead of leaning on bad company I learned to pray see, and my attitude changed instantly.

In a dusty tiny cabin in the wilderness I had a spiritual transformation out of terrible neediness.

PRESSURES OF AUTOIMMUNITY

The solution to all these problems was to find **ONE** man who loved me and marry him: protection.

It felt so good to come behind a wall! To say "bye bye y'all" and fly away from all the folderol.

No need to constantly explain myself to the dumbed, I have protection & understanding of **ONE**.

Get **ONE** man in your corner then work through him maintaining your sanity, poise and spirit.

That's the way it was always done and now more than ever or life is hard, exhausting and no fun.

I'm now done. You made me feel unsafe, comparing me to the mundane, inferior or the young.

I reject feeling framed by comparisons to others in your stable, fanbase, network--I'm done man.

NUMBER ONE OR FORGET IT

I'm number **ONE** or forget it, good bye. That's all I gotta say guy, these feelings are over, history.

Especially if she's younger, must now withdraw totally and go to **INNER** for exciting adventures.

Single I was a bull's eye attracting arrows from all sides. Married I'm happily respected with my guy.

Women get used to being attacked. Like a million cruel darts flying which they learn to deny in fact.

I tried dependency on female friends but that was even more abusive. Backstabbers and gossips.

The lowminded guys think younger is better until they grow up suddenly after inevitable disaster.

PRESSURES OF AUTOIMMUNITY

Think back with a clear mind to all the insults on your appearance, your age even your lovely face!

It's like they wanted to bring me down. Unable to do it verbally they just got mean/evil clowns.

Instead of inferior friends & bad marriage make peace with husband and drop phony entourage.

They don't believe in marriage and you're taking their advice? Drop these friends and go right.

LOYALTY IS COMPLETE CONFIDENTIALITY

Realize those leaking your personal business are not your friends. Demand loyalty or life's grim.

See that old and ugly whoremonger? That's the guy who insulted your looks when younger.

If they insult when with him they're trying to cuckold your husband. Take note/avoid from then on.

Above all, learn to identify subtle attacks. They think you're dumb so promptly disprove that.

You thought me so needy I'd stay in that matrix of treachery but it stops here, I'm free see.

For we are ALL sinners. You must vet em/not take em in so quickly, go slowly without blinders.

Withdraw from funny stuff [this debauchery] cuz it takes the rest of your life to get over it see.

PUTIN: THE HORROR OF BEDLAM

Putin is very big on not hurting historical or religious monuments but it's ok hitting apartments?

PRESSURES OF AUTOIMMUNITY

Obviously the time for diplomacy and sanctions have passed. Obviously we must stand against this.

Hubris Syndrome: Self-glory, obsession with image, contempt for advice, impulsive/reckless.

Hubris syndrome abates when the dictator loses power. His mental illness deflates in that hour.

Philosophy of Putin is Machiavellian. Don't merely injure your enemy, must utterly destroy them.

The Kalergi Plan is a browning of America. To make us controllable: all the same yet a darker shade.

THIRD PARTIES MAKE IT CRAZY

If it's just you two every day's a holiday but now add a third party and it all goes to hell speedily.

I never knew people like that existed. I guess in retrospect I had to go thru all that sis.

I know it's hard but transmute those experiences into greater resolve to represent the opposite.

Mom and dad never told me people were like this. It was such a shock but made me resist it.

Decency, civility, respect--where was it? It's the ontologically fatal insight, my world collapsed.

For people are cruel, be no one's mule. Have as your goal life behind a wall, now you walk tall.

I'm a very stable person. I may get miffed but it's all kept within range--no more a wild one.

The difficulties I experienced for years opened me up to higher spheres and gave me writing fodder.

PRESSURES OF AUTOIMMUNITY

CINDY THE LIBERAL WITCH

Liberal witches: They see what they wanna see and they rule their domain thru gossip/treachery.

Like most narcissists the liberal witches can't stand differences so you're their target sis.

The Jezebels don't just take down the dudes but get into female feuds and they're far more cruel.

She knew everyone's name—it was a "connectedness" game and she was always workin' it: blame.

She discussed me openly with everyone—they all knew my business—all the while acting innocent.

As my life took a nose dive I needed her more and she was there encouraging me to get worse.

The other female witches hate you just because they do, they don't need to explain it to you.

It's no longer a sisterhood welcoming society when you move to town, they meet to take you down.

HANDLING DIFFERENCES

It's with your differences that you'll see what a person is made of from the inside out: take notice.

With such low self-awareness combined with high need for flattery they just can't handle differences.

Does he seek to understand someone different, or does he shun them? These are valid markers.

Does he hear them out or instinctively invalidate them? To ascertain a narcissist ask these questions.

PRESSURES OF AUTOIMMUNITY

The narcissist isn't just a nuisance he can be very dangerous: phony, angry, calloused.

They are phony how they engage. They want that top position but you'll never know them ok.

If you like a certain trait, for awhile they'll go along with that but for longterm don't count on it.

There's an underlying simmering agitation ready to set them off and that's what you deal with.

That simmering anger is driven by strong imperative thinking: black or white, yes or no see.

The message: you'd better not deviate from me and if I'm angry your assertion is not an option.

When on slow simmer your differences don't matter but if on a boil they bring out the butcher.

Your differences are your genius but they are despised by the narcissist, remember that sis.

THEY HATE WHAT MAKES A GENIUS

Your unique differences make you great later but in childhood will get you beat up faster.

The more genius you are the more different on every nonverbal level from eye blinks to posture.

Who gets slaughtered by difference-haters? The genius or saint that's who-- and few make it to older.

Who can make it past these massive resistances to true genius? Only the saint relying on God sis.

I knew they couldn't understand me but nor was I apologetic--I was just afraid for my life.

PRESSURES OF AUTOIMMUNITY

She was mad every instant for all of my many differences: I was afraid she'd hit me miss.

On every level of the nonverbal hierarchy he is different from eye-blinks to posture/can't correct it.

MOMS WHO HATE THEIR DAUGHTERS

Her mother a narcissist hated her own daughter who was different and rebellious she'd insist.

When her daughter fell she'd gossip ruthlessly to all others even the neighbors about "her".

When angry they consciously choose to humiliate or to put people in their place in any case.

Can't just make things right with self-esteem intact, they gotta slay the victim and in public.

I got to where I never went out or always chaperoned when I did--attacked for being different.

Instead of conciliating it's "I'm gonna teach you a lesson you'll never forget"--he's dangerous honey.

They're just mean, period. Whether male or female they easily go on an anger-bender: great danger.

Stay away from these bummers or you'll be their victim sooner or later. It's a spirit, the destroyer.

So you have the phoniness--you'll never know me miss--combined with anger = most dangerous.

The most dangerous is the narcissist's hard, callous nature. The message is "I couldn't care less!"

They have no appreciation/understanding of "love". They demand respect but to love they scoff.

PRESSURES OF AUTOIMMUNITY

SENSITIVES WITH A CALLOUS MAN

I grew terrified of his callousness--what was he going to do next? He gained quick control by this.

If you're sensitive but with a callous man you're unequally yoked and life is a hellish bedlam.

What was he going to do to me, to the cats? He had already showed callousness to that.

In the female community being different can get em all against you at once. Odd girl out, dunce.

Instead of showing love/spreading good will they move towards bully characteristics forever still.

Callousness makes em impervious to the pain they caused you man/being tough's a badge.

They must leave their foes flattened and that's the bottom line--you're unequally yoked man.

He likes how he creates an intimidating presence. That's his thing, you can't talk him out of it.

Phoniness, anger and with callousness: This is your sign to get out, you're up against a nut.

When I escaped back to the warm desert in my little hut I was so relieved being free of a narcissist.

COLDBLOODED ENVIRONMENTS

That cold, bland, terrifying, unpredictable environment: now I knew the psychology of the aberrant.

Let's wrap this up by saying get a FIRM understanding of what you're dealing with here honey.

PRESSURES OF AUTOIMMUNITY

You'll try to bring in reason dealing with this person but these three traits destroy any such thing.

Not only is there no end to this it only gets worse increasingly sis and you could die of it.

A cruel, horrible little boy in a man's body. Someone with no lines when it comes to his enemy.

Get away from this little man and count yourself fabulously lucky/start your new life today.

Realize you're not gonna have a collaborative, caring or loving relationship with him, The End.

They lack introspection, self-reflection, correction. The only thing that works is consequences hon'

I learned from this. Instead of phoniness realness, anger for calmness, empathy for callousness.

CHECK THE ENVIRONMENT

It's true the world is femalecentric but that doesn't help a conservative woman at all, she's still hated.

What would you think hearing a woman say those things? Shocked/disgusted right? Well what about him?

With that Jezebel maid in the house it was like the household was rudderless/off course.

Is he a wonderful new addition or a big lug? Think about this before you encumber yourself.

Minimum relationship standards: he must see you, hear you and understand you/not all about him.

It's the minimum you require in order to engage your emotional attachment system, get it man.

PRESSURES OF AUTOIMMUNITY

We become people-pleasers to silence voices of shame. We're not good enough they're sayin'

The victim mentality is steeped in toxic shame. It can't make a move, doesn't have a goal, it's inane.

ENGAGING EMOTIONAL ATTACHMENT SYSTEM

From now on, before I engage my emotional attachment system I gotta vet you AND your dam friends.

ONE flip-flop/condescending word and I will instantly disengage my emotional attachment system.

Until they come to Jesus and individuate their intellect they're just a herd led by opinion leaders.

Men are bigger than women so of course I'm not gonna take it. Even one word and I'll escape it.

The test of truth is how many people DON'T come back vs. the popular peanut gallery of selfies flack.

She speaks the truth but has low presentation--it's boring. The incisive speaker is fascinating.

AVOID NAME-DROPPERS

My greatest antipathy is a name-dropper. Status thru association--who you know--is low/a faker.

He's seeking reflected glory from who he knows. He presumes friendship before it's bestowed.

Narcissist controlled all aspects of your life so by going no-contact that energy goes back inside.

By taking all that energy he controlled and putting it back into your own life you finally get over the guy.

PRESSURES OF AUTOIMMUNITY

Cuza what my sisters said they broke my windows and killed my dog. Calumny is terrible, pray to God.

Go ahead, if I'm that easily replaceable I couldn't care I less. Any value you certainly didn't recognize.

Devil makes it easy to hookup via internet but harder to get over ex--must include in no-contact.

Due to connection to Satan he looks good one day but lousy the next. He's inconsistent, just wait for it.

IS HE REALLY LISTENING?

When you say something and they tangentialize that's narcissism cuz they make it all about them.

When you say something and they spring into many different subjects that's also narcissism.

He's not truly listening to you if he springs off into other subjects. Tangentializing is frustrating.

The narcissistic female gets uncomfortable when you talk to her children and especially her husband.

They've got an attitude in their head that people should be just like them, that they are special.

SIGNS OF NARCISSISM IN YOUR LIFE

If your friend is narcissistic your success ticks him off. He finds excuses to marginalize you/ to mock.

If you're dealing with a narcissist in your life he's gonna expect you to change your plans, no strife.

It's like future faking: someone who makes promises and doesn't keep em, casual comments forgotten.

PRESSURES OF AUTOIMMUNITY

Acquaintances: If they aren't entirely cordial you put em in the outer circle. No getting close pal.

The promise to create/plan with you then they change the plan when you never saw a reason to man.

They can't honor their word & are constantly shifting. It's about what's happening in the moment darling.

A narcissist is all about one-upmanship and crazy communication keeping your focus on him.

The prophet's power was restricted in his own home and town due to dishonor/trying to bring him down.

If I've lived dishonorably I do/will repent but I'm not gonna stay in a room if dishonored by you/them.

If I've lived honorably and been a good Christian then I'm gonna make you honor me by separating.

While I didn't like his retaliation measures it gave me the oomph to claim my freedom that much more.

Change can be good. I don't need someone who comes against me simply because I wanna be me.

If I were immoral in some way it'd be different. But I've taken stock and this crap's unwarranted.

I escaped a narc before & it broke his heart. Not because he loved me but cuz it wasn't him who departed.

His retaliations were horrible/extreme and all I knew was I had to get outa there then, immediately.

WRONG INVOLVEMENTS AND ESCAPE

Get involved with someone wrong and your life's at stake. Never let your heart be broken by fakes.

PRESSURES OF AUTOIMMUNITY

It's when he senses you're trying to escape--cuz you see him for what he is--that things get dangerous.

Refuse to be controlled by that narcissist anymore and they'll show their pathology, guaranteed.

You must understand your shame is toxic crap passed on. It landed on you, you accepted it that's all.

When you were too weak to stand up against these projections from others all hell came in.

Who is the chosen scapegoat for this process in sick systems? The odd girl who is different?

Your mental illness was culture-based since it was morally debased. You didn't know in any case.

A frenemy wants a shortcut to your blessings. He wants to move in on whatever you got going.

A frenemy encourages unhealthy behavior and will always be there to help you self-sabotage for sure.

FRENEMIES ARE WEAK PEOPLE

A frenemy is a weak person and they always feel threatened--like by your other friends.

A frenemy uses passive-aggressive control tactics like the silent treatment which works with weakness.

A frenemy will turn against you in two instances: when you lose weight and when you get married.

If you have bigger dreams than other women you're sure to have a frenemy blocking what you're doin'.

He came into my life, lovebombed and discarded me--a trauma bond carrying a torch for treachery.

PRESSURES OF AUTOIMMUNITY

To say I'm busy--to lay boundaries down like that--takes years even decades but it equals success.

I'm filled with remorse but does that not mark the saint when all the others could not care less?

He's compelled to shit test you to test response. That's the narcissist but he brings himself down, alas.

PREVALENCE OF NARCISSISM

A frenemy will turn against you when you are now married and provided for when to men she's lost allure.

Why are narcissists everywhere? Because the cultural psychology has changed since the big war.

The **TEMPLATE** was genetic but **STRESS** was the breaking point making the crazy symptoms roll out.

You always lose yourself when you run behind someone else. In chasing a clown you've lost vision.

False soul ties based on deferred hope/sex perversions take you away from yourself and a future hon'

Fortunately a narc never apologizes cuz he'd hoover her back in instantly, this way she has a chance.

Youth aren't into things like guilt, shame, humiliation or repentance--it's all good don't you know that.

They are so horrible you must escape them now. Don't ever get into a car with them either, ciao.

One is in disbelief as he looks back to when due to trauma he had moral collapse but saints all feel that.

QUARANTINE: NO-CONTACT

PRESSURES OF AUTOIMMUNITY

You must quarantine from that virus: You gotta go no-contact on social media to get truly free sis.

This quarantine entails the work on your end of NOT GOING TO PAGES that evoke said chemicals.

You planted a giant seed now just wait. Recall there's always a period before blossoming ok.

Jezebel: You coulda been killed but God saved in time. Let her back in and you will be, no lyin.

You coulda been killed by characters you had in your life. They hate conservatives so prepare for strife.

They use smear campaigns against you, that's the main thing to remember in your game plan too.

Remorse for my past sins crippled me until I realized the others feel none of that sort of thing.

If allowing your dignity to be toyed with in a soul tie relationship, time is gone your biggest asset.

Why would swine trample pearls? Because they cannot discern value and he's equally dense girl.

Don't value connections where dignity is bashed and never forget soul ties are based on lust.

The danger of a soul tie: lost time, bashed dignity and your relationship availability is preoccupied.

God's not going to expose His good sons to you if you're preoccupied with a clown and sexual too.

HOOKED TO PERVERSION

As long as you're hooked to perverted soul ties you don't qualify. God won't put a King in your life.

PRESSURES OF AUTOIMMUNITY

You say it's secret/just in your thoughts but God still sees/hears and your life's still draining out.

Soul ties are based on spirit of LUST as time is wasted out and dignity is bashed in a confused mess.

Don't throw your pearls before swine or be trampled by them. He just can't discern your value man.

Your relational availability is preoccupied with a waste of time/a terrible bash to your self esteem, aye.

Make a decision to get this out of your life to step into what God really has for you if unpolluted.

With a polluted spirit you don't have joy, peace or a clear mind. He's always there so say goodbye.

There's a transference of spirits through sex. To be joined to a whore is a hellish life of strife and more.

The lady asked why she was so unhappy. She was engaging with the spirit of pollution, that's why.

Submit to God, repent of adultery and resist the devil so he will flee. Now God surely answers thee.

Cleanse your hands sinners and purify your hearts--everything that's not right like that tart.

The spirit of lust is a desire for something that's not yours. Pray only for a clean heart and seek the pure.

WILL POWER WON'T WORK

Hope deferred makes the heart sick but when he's nice again it breathes life into their false clique.

Will power won't be enough to break this bond. You need One thing at this point, the power of God.

PRESSURES OF AUTOIMMUNITY

Don't let your future spill out on the floor, dignity toyed with or spirit polluted: pray God ends this.

Facial recognition firm claims Antifa infiltrated Trump supporters who stormed capital that's all.

Facial recognition firm [XR vision] claims Antifa infiltrated Trump supporters who stormed the capital.

When these psychic toxins get into the soul they confuse life in ways that are unbelievable and cruel.

There are freed slaves who begged to go back into slavery because it was the familiar, just like her.

She is so attached to the familiar she allows her abuser to use up all her best years before discard.

The biggest reason for hanging on is fear of being alone sis: must learn to love and be fulfilled by it.

It's not love, it's an attachment to the familiar. Or fear of being alone or unattached as if it's weird.

It's not love but a soul tie/demonic attachment to another usually thru illicit sex and acting as a HEX.

Demonic men and women create soul ties without you knowing it, that's how you are conquered.

Women are intentionally making men into their puppets through soul ties/sex and what a racket.

HE'S GOT A SOUL TIE NOW...

He's got a soul tie now: As an ox to slaughter he's blindly led away as a cucked joker conquered.

He's got a soul tie now: by running behind that woman he will lose his life in what is wrongly call love.

PRESSURES OF AUTOIMMUNITY

You can't keep him in your bed and get him out of your head. Quarantine those thoughts/be led.

Demonic men/women create soul ties without you knowing it, that's how you easily become a dumb nut.

Jesus said we're blessed when they hate/throw us outa their company. It's a good sign not ignominy.

Why do we love people who don't love back? Number one: we're snared by rejection.

REJECTION IS A STRONGHOLD

Rejection is introduced in our lives while unaware of what's happening. Expecting love, it's excruciating.

By the time rejection has done it's work on our self-view it's re-arranged our internal settings to abnormal.

Rejection is a virus making us dysfunctional if you don't know: a template of destruction as it grows.

Rejection becomes a stronghold not just a temporary virus. It all adds up then our autoimmunity gives up.

Rejection depletes soul of all the antibodies necessary to fight the rejection off--that's lethal enough.

You have no right to even **TALK** to that man but instead he becomes a stronghold, a soul tie to a clown.

When alone I was productive, happy, spiritual, consistent. In a soul tie I was frantic, suicidal, suspicious.

God wants us to be paired up so if you stay alone/work on yourself gravitational pull becomes a magnet.

WE'RE NOT ALLOWED AUTO-IMMUNITY

PRESSURES OF AUTOIMMUNITY

Pressures of autoimmunity: You reacting all the time cuz everything is bad while they have seared consciences.

We're no longer allowed our auto-immune reactions to creeps. What used to be obvious is not to peeps.

Just because we discern they call us rigid evil haters. They think "all is -ONE" which is mental illness.

People didn't have to adapt to this before—it's exhausting and debilitating. Work on your immunity.

We won't accept it, we can't accept it. But they'll get you back if you think like that.

We draw lines, they do not. We are disgusted, they tolerate it all.

To be out of grace is to be on a crooked path. That's any sin (addiction) including to people, bad.

They called me angry hater cuz I had auto-immune reactions against the debauched witch on the block.

Just as I auto-react to wrong foods I react RIGHTLY to crude dudes but I'm called unloving by fools.

EVEN CHURCHES ARE SOCIAL JUSTICE WARRIORS

Society only acknowledges science which is politically correct--that race/gender are mere social constructs.

The federal government has ONE job: to protect us from foreign invaders—and they're not doing it.

Churches are the problem, they've fallen! They meet em at the border and ship em to red states to flip em.

They seek social justice at the expense of truth. For an empirical scientist in this generation it's cruel.

PRESSURES OF AUTOIMMUNITY

As Overton Window is kicked hard left, a "progressive" isn't regarded anymore as a radical communist.

They've prevented our gut reactions to things. Which are HORRIFIC, we never saw anything like it.

Victory is when you've finally pushed em all away, all those Dunning-Krugers seeking to advise you, ok?

He even looks like a "Dunning Kruger": someone who thinks he's smart but isn't, a mere technician.

SOMNAMBULANT SPIRITS: YOU ASK *THEM*?

His somnambulant spirit was so heavy I felt like going to sleep and escaped his dominance, was free.

It's way too sophisticated for them yet you're asking for their opinion? Get a grip/don't respect humans.

The crooked path: Sin brings total disorder in self, body, system and everyone who touches em.

Sin separates us from self and God. It's an awful place after partying with the mob/going along with stuff.

Knowing I don't have to please anyone except that ONE is so relieving. I'm getting high anticipating.

Tho' God called her to be a prolific author she got distracted into decades of dung thinking she's awful.

MEMORIES ARE SATAN'S ANCHORS

It's not just PTSD that triggers memories, it's Satan who wants you ANCHORED to that crap last century.

I always saw people as an encumbrance. They worship you one moment then go to war on you the next.

PRESSURES OF AUTOIMMUNITY

He keeps you in obscurity before releasing you to notoriety. Just like God did to Moses in the desert for 40.

God is the one who positions you and everything is perfect timing, so give up on people honey.

It's all timing, WAIT on the Lord. I say again: It's all timing, WAIT on the Lord. And again: It's all timing, WAIT on the Lord.

They saw nothing wrong with the crude slut cuz she said she's good tho' no morals and a heart of wood.

It was such an emotional and mental draught that I clung to sensual appetites just to have my own thoughts.

Pressures of autoimmunity: Like being a cat in a room full of rocking-chairs.

Autoimmunity: a new level of dietary restraint. Fruitarians eat rice, we can't. We can eat fish, they wouldn't.

WE MAL-ADAPT TO PEOPLE THRU MENTAL ILLNESS

You don't save someone from quicksand by jumping in yourself. wise saying

I mal-adapted all over the place (illness) to the liberal mindset or how they imposed on my space.

I didn't know the liberal ambience was killing me just that I was miserable in life itself--how could I know?

Quit complaining about what they did to you and only ask: why didn't you see it before/why were they there?

You're either with me, against me or in my way.

The preparatory stage is dealing with people who don't understand you, building barriers too.

Quit complaining about these people when all your friends saw em for what they were, evil.

PRESSURES OF AUTOIMMUNITY

Quit complaining about these people when at one time you too were filled with the devil.

Instead of complaining about your guests ask: why in hell did you ever invite in these pests?

Instead of telling me to be happy in my new home they said "you made it out of Borrego"

All I know is, I coulda been killed but wasn't because God my Father was present.

What I've learned from years studying it: Humans comply with the mob to avoid being targeted by it.

IT'S NOT BRAVE TO COLLECTIVELY GANG UP

They're called "brave" when collectively ganging up on someone or being soothed by fake adulation.

Political correctness has built a snitch culture and a social justice industry based on spying/surveillance.

Left cries for "family cohesion" at the border yet a child's need for both parents leaves em unconcerned.

California times fifty is how the Democrats will have permanent political power.

It is blatant contradiction which drives us crazy or into mad outbursts seemingly "out of nowhere".

The system can't take so much contradiction without release, energy's gotta go somewhere.

Thought I could have her around tho' I knew she was wrong but she'd always bring me down.

Liberals can't debate so they always run away.

Pets have been killed in border towns by crossers. America was a decent country, can't you see this?

PRESSURES OF AUTOIMMUNITY

It's Sunday--you're just supposed to survey your work. Look it over, revel in it, enjoy your day and pray.

All the pets have been killed along the border. How can you be so cruel you democrat consenters

DEMOCRATS DON'T CARE ABOUT CRIME OR PEOPLE

The democrats don't care about the crime or brutal savagery on Americans and their pets.

Third world cultures don't care about cats and dogs, wherever poverty prevails it is naught.

It doesn't matter what they say, you know it's the best, ok?

If you're stuck in unrepentant sin He's gonna withdraw, being a Gentleman He won't force it.

Just one day a week, Sunday--to do nothing but praise Him. Take the whole day to see afar, amen.

During the week we get busy cuz we're workers for the Lord so we assure ONE day for the amazing.

Praise God for His works that come through me which I review every Sunday.

THE DEVIL OR THE SYSTEM?

Looking back it had to be the devil or the system--the system IS the devil and the devil USES systems.

My system was interlocking jealousy patterns, contradictions and double binds in herds.

The women [pack jealousy] attacked me as the newcomer upstart and it was scary these tarts.

It drove me wild--out of control til I learned with a new style adapting to the rank and file.

PRESSURES OF AUTOIMMUNITY

All of women's baser emotions--jealousy, crass competitiveness, cattiness--come out of them.

Psalms 1: they group against God's anointed vowing to bring him down but God laughs at em.

In unenlightened communist eras if you're too big they'll kill you: Satan steals, kills and destroys.

Just do your work in silent devotion to it and don't talk about it--manage the communist spirit.

The communist spirit is most prevalent with women who want big government and open borders.

THE COMMUNIST SPIRIT IS FAKE EMPATHY

The communist spirit sucks its power from empathy, feelings and emotion which are feminine.

But it's contradictory empathy since they downgrade the family constantly let alone morality.

He'll take you from the background to the foreground, from being overlooked to being in charge, amen!

They blame the homeless crisis on capitalism rather than democrat policies in the "elite" coastal cities.

Hearing youth talk is frightening and disgusting, a reason to panic or demand they teach Civics.

Judging from all the crazy things I did under the devil's influence I certainly can't judge you Sis.

It's not about teaching pedophilia to the kids but normalizing ALL perversions starting with that.

AS SOON AS you give up petty plans and stabs in the dark God takes over putting you on the mark.

PRESSURES OF AUTOIMMUNITY

It's hard waiting when there's no indication of a thing--in fact nothing--but it's just a test sweetie.

Never eat unless hungry. Fasting is healing and makes you cosmic and spiritual while waiting.

You know God was behind your work, you felt it in the groove. He also has the link for it, He's so cool!

You can tell by their reactions to things whether they're good or bad, reasonable or democrat.

THEY MOCK AND SCOFF AT YOUR VIEWS

Wicked will smirk, laugh and scoff at your views. Learn to expect it, be warm steel, stay removed.

Wicked will laugh at you as if they're superior. That's the way it's been for decades but have no fear.

Liberals strive to look happy. It's all about giddy approval of those in their echo chamber but still a tragedy.

It's all about cheesecake, showing their teeth, syrupy affection and kissing em on the cheek, ICK!

Liberals long to show you how happy they are but in reality their evil stands on things are sickest by far.

The enemy says it's over but God says it's just the beginning of your new life. Dust off your dreams, revive!

They lied on me, spread false rumors, got everyone against me: I took it as a sign God loves me, truly.

My sisters plotted and planned my demise, my destruction. They planted evil seeds but I still loved em.

It's hard loving those so boastful and arrogant but know they bring themselves down without any doubts.

PRESSURES OF AUTOIMMUNITY

God called you to bear much fruit. You are a chosen people, even before birth He saw you were cute.

Born clear, we mal-adapt to the system that awaits us: getting back to the True Self is difficult.

She woke up thinking she was awful—Satan gets us in the mornings with his insults and falsehoods.

ALL OF MY mistakes I'd wake up to. The same ones over and over caused anxiety and self-disgust too.

BEST BECOMES WORST, WORST BECOMES BEST

The best becomes worst, the worst the best: That's a human archetype to recall to give you ZEST.

The best are the most sensitive so when things go wrong they can really do some damage--I did I guess.

When the sensitive suffer hurt they venture to the darkness unprotected and it's scary, destructive, death.

In utter weakness the sinner is compelled to do those things as the devil really makes him do it.

The weak suffer autonomisms: uprushes from the unconscious which is evil and endlessly senseless.

Tattoos? CHECK. Buzzwords like diversity? CHECK. Virtue signaling but hating Trump? CHECK.

GOD'S PECULIAR PEOPLE

To be "PECULIAR" means you are set apart, chosen, sanctified before the earth, chosen by God himself.

Devil's Horns hand sign: CHECK. Screaming, kissing, hugging girlfriends: CHECK. Your reaction: ICK!

PRESSURES OF AUTOIMMUNITY

Prolonged, magnified and silly reactions to things and jumping up and down: Millennial children.

Teen rapper: Jumping up and down like an idiot--this is your rap star? So boring and immature!

I'd rather use my name from birth and explore my Latin side, not change my name to Latin when I'm not.

How to know you're chosen: YOU DON'T FIT! You will feel like a misfit until you find your purpose.

I didn't fit 'til I found Him.

Mis-fits develop a deep hunger for God. Being disadvantaged becomes a great advantage for the odd.

I didn't fit the contestants in the family lineup--their status-tension and aggression I'd had my fill of.

WHEN THE LAST CHRISTIAN DIES

When the last Christian patriarch died the family was taken over by evil offshoots though rich.

When the patriarch died the vacuum was filled with multicultural liberals without God, religion or morals.

Don't look east or west for success: God's the one who positions you, lifts you up, shuts and opens doors.

What made me hungry for the Lord was being disadvantaged: being left out in the field, ignored.

Without faith [that God has the link] it is impossible to please Him [so better get your faith back, quick.

If God said you're gonna be the head you'll be the head and not the tail--His promises never fail.

PRESSURES OF AUTOIMMUNITY

If God said you'd flourish in Your Season, prepare for that cuz it's your whole reason for livin'.

From a ghost-town I became hungry for the Lord. You can't teach people hunger, I had to overcome.

It worked something outa me, something I didn't know was there, when you treated me so unfair.

Thank you: Because of what you put me thru I learned God was GREATER than my enemies so now I bid adieu.

Vulgar people imposing on me: lowly, grabby, tyrannical when getting the upper hand, losers/time-wasters.

It was GOOD being imposed on for years so I'd learn boundaries and VERY HIGH WALLS free of tears.

IT WAS GOOD I WAS BASHED: THINK THAT

It was GOOD that I was bashed cuz I ran my mouth too much in arrogance--in restraint I can have sass.

I was harassed on every side, became weak in my body, wanted to die until to God I cried.

Stoning is the principal of one thing after another as the potter forms the clay to withstand whatever.

It's in darkness that God's spirit begins to move. You can't see, you're exhausted, you're confused.

It's whenever things are chaotic that God's spirit begins to move. He is a God of order as chaos dissolves.

In my darkest hour I hit a vein: a vein gushing with glory, redemption, the goodness of God. Job

Comeback kid: Because there's a spirit inside you that comes back when they thought you were dead.

PRESSURES OF AUTOIMMUNITY

Don't get discouraged because God keeps you in hiding--He keeps you in obscurity before unveiling.

For if you go public too early, they will kill you. Wait for your set time, God has it planned to last detail.

It was like I was in bootcamp and God had hired those demons to teach me what I needed to know.

It's GOD who opens doors. So stop your petty stabs in the dark and relax--you need SOLITUDE more.

Your spouse may forget what you did, but the Lord's not unrighteous to forget your labor of love!

God said: "Karen, I saw every time you wrote a verse to de-confuse or destroy a curse and I will reimburse."

THINGS MUST GET WORSE TO GET BETTER

Sometimes things have to get worse before they get better--that's so you'll depend on your Father.

Non-issues, side issues, distractions, tangents and irrelevants: that's the lower mind of sinners/miscreants.

Women's show "The View" is catty, narrow, dogmatic, social and cruel--remind you of anyone you knew?

Dominate, create! Don't cower in bad faith in the third-rate. YOU are it, God created your great destiny.

NEVER rely on people. Block em all or they'll lead you down rabbit holes which are circuitous, lethal, evil.

Pay no mind to any of them, they are useless. They just think they're a big deal cuz that's how it always is.

The day starts at midnight. You could never appreciate daybreak without going thru this dark blight.

PRESSURES OF AUTOIMMUNITY

Persecution was good for me for how else could I learn God's perfect protection or what it means to be free?

They raked me over coals and whether deserved or not, I understand it's a phase/part of the process.

Being imposed on was good for me for how else could i see a need for the HIGHEST boundaries?

Being bored to death was good for me for how else could I discover what I think and say was best?

Get into the car, you're under their control. The mishaps from this got old. Never again, I'll stay home.

It's not by your ears but your spirit going beyond the natural to the voice of God anchoring your soul!

DEPENDENCY BRINGS FORCED REMOVAL

If you're too addicted to someone or dependent on their bloody approval God is forced to remove em.

If you need the approval of your bloody echo chamber suddenly reality will hit that you were in error.

I thank God for the awful, horrible lessons proving the need for a hard line, hard-won line on morality.

I thank God for the hard lessons proving the most important thing other than self-defense is PRIVACY.

We must resurrect the frontier mentality: Not trusting strangers and developing in privacy.

In the fifties LATIN cocktail music was very popular but then after the Beatles we lost it, forever?

The more sensitive you are the more crazy you'll go under liberal rule. You have a heart/conscience, not a fool.

PRESSURES OF AUTOIMMUNITY

By following the autoimmune protocol [AIP] I can more easily handle chemicals/what comes.

Rejection gives direction in your life. Paula White

I didn't give you any more than you could stand or less than you needed to learn the lesson. The Lord

They keep trying to demoralize patriots with their anti-American garbage which is violent, my gosh.

Not just demoralized but discouraged when all are dumbed down or don't care, what of the future?

Hmm, guess I had to go thru ALL THAT--which as beyond horrible--to see the need for boundaries.

ON THOSE NOT SEEING A NEED FOR WALLS

I was so naive and trusting I didn't even see a need for a fence and a locked gate--an earlier American age.

Early America: Porches not fences cuz everyone co-mingles, it's ok if they dawdle, we trust em all.

Borrego 1970's architecture: porches, no fences, everyone's together in a neighbor join-us communitas.

Most Borrego homes are second homes--without fences they'll be taken over by squatters soon.

It's not a matter of how could they be so bad, but what were you doing with such immature cads?

I'd get burned out/ready to give up, then I'd recall the synchronistic FIRE of the Creative Act/can't stop.

When the whole comes together like a jigsaw puzzle you KNOW it's God--recall that while waiting/off.

PRESSURES OF AUTOIMMUNITY

If you have a problem with needing people's approval (getting high or low) God removes it ya know.

She was so gross imposing on me I felt like a victim but with knowledge of the situation I took domination.

Famous people are walled in so take that as a lesson and change your position--you'll be glad you did.

Quit thinking back to prior eras (lower levels)--it's counterproductive since it's fighting nonexistent devils.

You'd never be in that position again (you've evolved and learned) so why go back and get burned?

BONDS AND TRIGGERS OF OLD SYSTEMS

The bonds and triggers of old systems are powerful and inextricable and must be transcended to be well.

Low IQ means can be MEAN since RESTRAINT requires intelligence just as gentile refinement does.

Lesson of the ages: STAY AWAY. Once whole again reconnect to higher systems for synchronicity.

They're killing patriots--those who aren't mind-swept into globalist cosmology: "we are one" and other lies.

The false vision seems self-evident to those stricken. The "We are one" thing is the main problem.

The democrats have become a silly party of fake outrage and social engineering. Bill Maher

it's all gushy emotional privileged women kissing and hugging--it's rather sickening let alone boring

Crybaby authoritarian clowns have taken over the public square and if we dare criticize we're called haters.

PRESSURES OF AUTOIMMUNITY

FAVOR is heaven's kiss, God's endorsement. It's how we go from this season to our predestined position.

Favor puts you in a position with a Boaz who makes you filthy rich overnight.

FAVOR gives you undeserved access to the right person at the right time by the clever God of mine.

Favor: sovereign set-ups, divine connections, opportunities, open doors, moments set by God.

It's when all the earth groans that becomes a set-up for your appearance to move em into destiny.

His deliverance in your life will show the people the deliverance in theirs: the exemplar's fullness.

FAVOR IS THE ESTABLISHED TIME

Favor is the set time for God to stoop down and to bestow favor upon you by granting your request.

All the lessons and blocks overcome in your life is mirrored in what they're about to confront, ole.

God brings change IN you to create change in the earth, that's how it works so get ready/prepare.

Since you've been raised up for such a time as this, favor causes God to grant a "yes" to your request.

Favor grants the Elect privileges and positions even by ungodly authorities no matter how lousy.

If it's part of your destiny you can't lose it and if it isn't you can't gain it.

Barrenness means you can't produce it yourself, you're empty. It all comes from God almighty.

A move of God begins with barrenness to usher in new seasons: being emptied so God can use us.

PRESSURES OF AUTOIMMUNITY

We have to get outa the way cuz God moves in **EMPTINESS**. That's why vacuity equals **PROFITS**.

This is why John said "I must decrease so that He can increase."

True repentance brings the humbling necessary for destiny since it makes us duck to get out of His way.

How it works: I lower myself under the hand of God so that in **DUE SEASON** He lifts me up.

God's army in the latter days comes outa the crevices of darkness as He raises positions of the lowly.

FORGET MAN, GOD DOES THE LIFTING

So forget man, God is the one doing the lifting! Who? Those who have been in valleys, hurting!

Favor is God's endorsement--His OIL which flows and makes things incredibly easy, amen.

God always pulls us out of valleys to lift us up. If you're going through anything heavy, that's it.

Favor means the difficult mountain comes down in the presence of what God is doing in your town.

GRACE causes restoration and me to prosper when everyone else is losing or caught in capers.

Favor brings change, it comes to bring that mountain down. God is rescuing, His path is holy.

We become cleansed for His purposes. So why fear lack of success? He won't forget His servants.

God hates a proud look: Those who overestimate themselves while others are disdained and forsook.

PRESSURES OF AUTOIMMUNITY

She thought so highly of herself and down one me. A superior witch who put me in the ditch.

Never bemoan hard lessons of God. That was your training for what's ahead and now you won't stall.

Left-wing companies now control the tools of political debate and will even tell you who to hate.

By doing this you shift seasons into divine alignment. Now we will see the glory, imagine that.

Never bemoan (stink with resentment) hard lessons of God—He HAD to cleanse you of your flaws.

YOU HAD TO GO THRU IT *ALL!*

Everything you've gone through is preparation for a new season so never curse your crisis friends.

Joseph's bros hated him: Seeing what they hate about you brings understanding of your value.

You had to go through what you did so that God could raise you up for such a time as this.

God uses brokenness to birth greatness. It's like a bow and arrow: It pulls way back then finds the targets.

Social media giants are digitally disappearing dissidents--great thinkers like Alex Jones for instance.

Many want the gift of evangelism since it means rockstar status but if you have it you just wanna give it.

An evangelist is totally different from a pastor or teacher. He has separate gifts to draw in the sinners.

If you're born an evangelist there's nothing you can do about it and you even got locked up for it.

PRESSURES OF AUTOIMMUNITY

Those qualities and talents of an evangelist gotta go somewhere and if kept inside he's a stutterer.

You GOTTA DO IT no matter how old. Health problems no excuse with modern tech so BE BOLD.

Families are a small sovereign unit that should form a barrier against corruption taking over.

Whenever the wrath of God is unleashed on sick societies what first happens is a sex revolution.

Wrath of God signs: Romans 1: 24 a sex revolution, then a homo revolution led by lesbians. Roman 1: 26.

Signs of God's wrath being unleashed: the reprobate mind. The thinking is so corrupt it can never unwind.

MUST SPEAK TRUTH TO REPROBATE MINDS

It is not proper to speak of anyone disparagingly but that means we can't ever tell the truth honey.

The reprobate mind results from the sex revolution justifying sin and the confused thoughts therein.

Depraved minds mean everything improper happens: wickedness, greed, envy, strife, gossip and slander.

Signs of God's wrath being unleashed: the reprobate mind. Thinking is corrupt, distorted, gross, unrefined.

There isn't a supreme court justice who doesn't know what the bible says about it but they affirm it anyway.

God is pleased by our perseverance in the face of inevitable persecutions which seem to be constant.

Have mercy on us oh Lord for we are exceedingly filled with contempt. Psalms 123: 4

PRESSURES OF AUTOIMMUNITY

Our soul is exceedingly filled with scorn of those who are at ease, with the contempt of the proud.

Depart from Me to eternal fire: Jesus preached judgement always: that's compassionate and loving.

We're just passing through here so don't get hung up.

Mundaneity: Many of your memories, remorses and resentments could be the opposite to reality.

Did your sisters hate your guts cuz you're a filthy mutt or cuz you wouldn't adapt to their stuff?

So often the human animal takes rejection as a sign of unworthiness and a painful stigma may last.

TRUTH NOT BASED ON FANS AND FOLLOWERS

Free speech which is first rate: Every single topic you should be able to intellectually debate.

Truth is not based on the amount of followers, far from it. It relieves the Elect but the rest hate it.

Satan lies to billions. Or do you mean a stadium filled with seekers means the speaker is holy? Never.

If the amount of followers indicates a man of God, then what would you say of Jesus who only had 12?

Those that lead cause you to err.

As to my people, children are their oppressors and women rule over them. Isiah 3: 12

The heart becomes darkened when God is abandoned, then God abandons the darkened heart.

When God abandons a society it becomes pornographic first off--obsessed with sex.

PRESSURES OF AUTOIMMUNITY

CYCLES ALL THRU HISTORY

Cycle all through history: God abandons a nation then there's a sex revolution then a HOMO revolution.

God turns inveterate sinners over to a depraved mind--that's a mind that can't function or think right.

The biggest characteristic of the depraved mind is they become haters of God, their world a ball of mud.

Sequence: Sex revolution, homosexual revolution then the reprobate mind unleashing murder etc.

Its not love but HATE speech to affirm them and not warn them. It is LOVE to warn em of the hell comin'

Neither fornicators, homosexuals, drunkards nor swindlers will inherit the Kingdom of God.

The church is a collection of former idolaters, adulterers, fornicators, the effeminate and swindlers.

A BRAND NEW WORLD WITHOUT LOGIC

We're coming into a brand new world where logic is a menace/truth is the enemy and its scary.

The left loves tyranny when they're in control. They love death camps called re-education too.

They wanna live in a universe of what they want. Not true reality but some worldview, vision, narrative.

They don't believe in good, they don't even believe in evil. They only believe in raw control. Alex Jones

The mean cops enforcing covid laws are women. They come to your home treating you like vermin.

PRESSURES OF AUTOIMMUNITY

It makes no sense dragging people outa their homes to protect em from neighbors and themselves.

The universe leans towards justice because the imprint of God's law is there in just about all of us.

NOT BORN THAT WAY

It's NOT a genetic fluke or defect. You were this way, but are not anymore, whether thief or whore.

Everything is now being genetically blamed. Even fornicators have it inborn like they have no say in it.

If it's all genetic then why not have lobbies for all the sinners since they are born as homos or swindlers.

It would be hateful of me to affirm that terrible sin and loving to call for repentance and home again.

Homos are about one percent of the pop but 70% of murderers cuz it unleashes these horrors.

Quakers (another false church): "Homosexuality is no more deplorable than left-handedness".

Homo-affirmation is the worst hate speech. Tell him of his sin so he can be saved you creeps!

A man who puts on a woman's clothing is an abomination to the Lord your God. Deut. 22: 5

You don't like being in the "wrong body" but being a man or woman is the body God gave you Sparky.

How you can tell a society is abandoned: God spews it out because there's homos all around.

I'm telling your these things outa love not hate: for these sensual sins there's a high price to pay.

PRESSURES OF AUTOIMMUNITY

First God abandons it (SPEWS IT OUT) and then He destroys it (He has FINALLY had enough).

GOD'S JUDGMENT FRIGHTENING AS IT FALLS ON A COUNTRY

Sodomy and baby-killing make our land blood guilty and ripe for the consequences, a tragedy.

They came as aliens and already they're our judge.

It is preposterous to call them gay. Homosexual is clinical, sodomite is biblical, sinners is theological.

It is a horrible thing this sin, and a horrible thing for people to advocate it as normal. John MacArthur

Their face gives them away: they're sinners and they are BLATANT sinners and not just in aura.

Their oppressors are children. They're so weak even a child or usually the women rule over them!

It's a deadly sin, always a defining sin and damning sin that destroyed Sodom, Judah, Greece then Rome.

Calling it a sickness first then advocating it as superior (not worst) puts us on the brink of judgement.

The issue: They not only do the same but give hearty approval to those who do them--P-U!

Lord, an entire party in the USA has given hearty approval to these abominations, amen!

An entire party in the USA has given hearty approval to these abominations-- Lord, come again!

Sorest losers ever: they end friendships over Trump winning, call us bigots, unfriend on facebook.

PRESSURES OF AUTOIMMUNITY

Why does a society become obsessed with sex when God abandons it? Proliferate before it's too late!

We must speak the truth to rescue the perishing, not fill em with more gay pride and call it loving.

GLYCATION DIET FOR VANITY

Low glycation means low wrinkles. Believe it or not, most people don't care about this.

Forget the roasted tomatoes and garlic. It's high glycation along with broiling, grilling or frying.

Roasted tomatoes/garlic: It's delicious and I love it too but suffered for days. Glycation is what it is.

It's not the shrimp so much as the shrimp farms. The situation is dirty so sound the alarm.

The absolute best thing you can do for yourself today is take it off. No more work, relax in thought.

I am surrounded by five cats and two dogs and it's the highest I've ever been and closest to God.

AUTOIMMUNE REACTIONS TO FOODS

If you have autoimmune problems--if you're always in reaction--you must have a protocol to control it all.

Suffered depletion as a fruitarian so included lacto: not autoimmune protocol so now it's fish/fruit.

Fruit/avo most of the time, fish occasionally to prevent deficiencies--this seems perfect to me.

80% of immunity is in the gut so to avoid reactions we delete whole food categories.

Deleting grains, dairy, nightshades and citrus leaves: fruit, veggie and fish.

PRESSURES OF AUTOIMMUNITY

Ray tends to rely on pills and potions but as to the food/diet relationship to health he sees no connection.

To stop leaky gut you gotta delete whole categories of food: dairy, grains, nightshades, citrus--good!

With leaky gut you have S-H-I-T going through the bloodstream then locating on the skin: think of that!

To stop leaky gut {CLEAN THE BLOOD] I'd do anything since it means looking sweet/pure not like MUD.

Get off the GLUTEN thing because leaky gut comes as much from non-gluten grain sources which suk.

If you want fecal matter all over your face continue to eat your nightshades and grains--study this case.

Tomatoes, cheese and pepperoni make the gut look like PIZZA as fecal comes through holes: I'm appalled.

The bulimic may not even know what she's doing just a subconscious knowing that most food is poison.

NO GRAINS, DAIRY, NIGHTSHADES, CITRUS, LAND ANIMAL

Autoimmune Protocol: No grains, non-gluten grains, dairy, nightshades or citrus not even lemon on fish.

Leaky gut diet of fruit, veg and fish, who can do this? Those sick of s--* on their face.

May have to go lowcarb paleo for my autoimmune protocol. High-sugar fruits like grapes: gained lbs.

With such high green nutrition I'm never hungry but with the high-sugar fruits a little puffy.

Morning drink: kale, banana and berries. Lunch: foods of the seas. Dinner: never if you please. START

PRESSURES OF AUTOIMMUNITY

Sometimes I lose God, either from something I did or someone I was around or I ate wrong.

You need the greens so just put kale, berries and banana in blender for breakfast meal.

Pesca-Fruitarianism: fish and fruit is ultra-digestible, fibers like broccoli (with ANTI-NUTRIENTS) are NOT!

Carnivores eat fruit and leaves to varying degrees but I'll never eat those monsters again: the veggies--just leaves.

I can sure see why kids love ice cream and hate veggies--humans love creamy things not these.

The last time I ate broccoli I thought I'd die as the bowl of nails just sat there with anti-nutrients--I cried.

Fish is SO ultra-digestible compared to broccoli for example. Fish/fruit makes sense to be cute.

Leaves are different, they digest. Even nuts are better than those cruciforms and all the rest.

KIDS ARE RIGHT TO HATE VEGGIES

Mom made me sit there til I ate my vegetables--I sat there all night determined not be miserable.

I just cannot digest vegetables cooked or raw, period. To devise such a torture is beyond hideous.

I was sick as a lacto-fruitarian from the autoimmune response to dairy. I switched to fish: healthy.

What I'm against are vegans who get plastic surgery--botox and fillers to sell the false diet to followers.

Vegans past their prime get botox fillers to cover the sunken eyes characteristic of vegans with time.

PRESSURES OF AUTOIMMUNITY

Whatever the solid food I have reactions of autoimmune so now's the time for smoothies, grapes, juice.

Fruit, green smoothies and occasional fish--the most digestible not veggies impossible to digest.

Gave all my organic veggies to the neighbors. Just spinach or kale in smoothies, grapes: favor.

That broccoli I had was like a bowl of nails in the gut and it just sat there: what a lesson, clean sweep.

Be fruitarian MOST the time then have some fish once in awhile = NO DEFICIENCIES, young style.

There's pesca-fruitarian (fish) or lacto-fruitarian (dairy) but with autoimmune you can't have that.

AUTOIMMUNE REACTIONS TO EGGS OR DAIRY

There's also ovo-fruitarian (eggs) but with autoimmune you can't have that either so fish is the answer.

What a relief to know that with autoimmune I can't eat dairy, grains, nightshades, citrus or red meat.

What a relief to know exactly what the problem was! So common triggers: tomatoes, potatoes, citrus!

And by deleting those foods--done in an hour--I could finally take control of my health, feeling power!

AUTOIMMUNE REACTIONS TO STARCH

NO STARCH with autoimmune. I recall the body shooting acid at the bread/wanted to be dead.

No "anti-gluten" grains either, so get offa that thing. ALL grains even your daily oats in the morning.

PRESSURES OF AUTOIMMUNITY

Who could constrain their diet like this? Someone who's sick of seeing fecal matter on the face.

LEAKY GUT is what it's called and these foods are the culprits of these holes from gut to blood.

BEANS: lentils are the biggest culprit in leaky gut. While healing, stop problem foods for a month.

I felt so much better as my skin cleared, the gut streamlined, acid reflux was FINALLY gone, I felt joy.

I can't even have lemon on my fish cuz it triggers autoimmune response and leaky gut, so be it.

Those without autoimmune can enjoy orange juice, oatmeal, french fries, pizza, cheese, milk, beef.

But I will never put that crap in me again--to suffer ALL NIGHT LONG: praying, crying, burping.

Dizzy spells are leaving slowly. I hear clarity of mind is down the road but even so life is really fine.

I can't imagine living on beef. I know the carnivore diet works for some but I can't float like a leaf.

Fruit, leaves and fish: just seems purer. It's higher paleo and along with fasting it would be it were it not for dirt.

I'll be attacked by Freelee for eating fish but don't forget the Savior was a fisherman, a symbol enough.

The cleaner I get the more a handful of grapes makes a meal with full satiety and avo finishes it.

Since I changed diet why should you listen to me? Cuz you can eat those things if no autoimmune disease.

TOTAL LOAD AND AUTOIMMUNITY

PRESSURES OF AUTOIMMUNITY

With autoimmune, digestion adds too much to **TOTAL LOAD** and therefore you degrade {prince to toad}.

Ok we gotta have greens--just put em in the blender with your early morning smoothies.

We're not into eating just doing the job for greatest nourishment of the body and preventing deficiencies.

Morning smoothie: berries, coconut milk, nut butter, kale or spinach. Grapes, avo or fish: **BRUNCH**.

I got into her car and the frenemy purposely took me through toxic chemicals to prove I wasn't allergic at all.

Vegetables are advanced on autoimmune protocol [AIP] but with the anti-nutrients, how could that be?

One result of food poisoning is feelings of imminent doom. So the allergic are both sick and neurotic too.

Skinny people live ten years longer than others. Drop the load at the end and the end is extended.

Everyone knows that BIG beings die early. Whatever the species bigness is too high-maintenance.

Husband lost fifty pounds and entered a wider spiritual world, a perceptual phantasmagoria.

TO ART AND SCIENCE DISCOVERERS

WAIT to be discovered and remember there's only **ONE** link which a Holy God predesignated. **START**

At first a true discovery won't be received but be totally rejected, scorned, banned and censured.

The more people against it the more its truth value since a discovery's whole purpose is to break thru.

PRESSURES OF AUTOIMMUNITY

A discovery's purpose is to shatter obdurate mind concepts and the result is relief and moving up.

For the herd (the bell shaped curve) the thing is mundaneity--maintaining the same and no novelty.

Every culture has it's own mundaneity, road map or mental mazeway. If different, watch out baby.

The moral majority of public opinion is treated like a minority, a mental illness or sideshow on TV.

It's the Culture of Demonization if you voice these beliefs which comes at you like an energy thief.

The discoverer is lone thinker, that's his function but meanly mocked before his time has come.

WAITING is an actual phase of the Creative Act *after it's completion.*

Milestone: I have only 250 more pages to write to complete the *new 2021 prefaces* in 130 books.

The word DISCOVERY is a technical term--it must meet certain requirements like this work here.

100 KAREN KELLOCK BOOKS

KAREN KELLOCK PH.D.

M.S. Political Science, San Diego State. Ph.D. in Psychology, University of California Irvine. Postdoctoral: UCI School of Medicine, Dept. of Psychiatry [NIMH Grants]. Developed the Debris Theory of Disease, a theory of system pathology in 120 books and 22 textbooks for the general public. The theory has a general formula: All disease is obstruction, all recovery is elimination, all success is attraction. The three obstructions are people, habit and food. Remove obstruction and snap to your goals, waiting in the wings.